Minute Motivators for Teens

Stan Toler

G000055360

BEACON HILL PRESS

OF KANSAS CITY

Copyright © 2004, 2011, 2014 by Stan Toler

Beacon Hill Press of Kansas City
PO Box 419527
Kansas City, MO 64141
www.BeaconHillBooks.com

ISBN 978-0-8341-3287-0

Printed in the
United States of America

Library of Congress Control Number: 2014937912

The Internet addresses, email addresses, and phone numbers in this book are accurate at the time of publication. They are provided as a resource. Beacon Hill Press of Kansas City does not endorse them or vouch for their content or permanence.

10 9 8 7 6 5 4 3 2 1

Introduction

As if school wasn't hard enough, you're expected to excel in life as well!

In a world with more ups and downs than a roller-coaster ride, you need something that will help you stay focused. This is it. From the classroom to the gym to the job site, *Minute Motivators for Teens* offers some principles for tackling life like an NFL linebacker.

Like it or not, the days of our lives aren't like a computer game. We don't always know the outcome, and sometimes there are glitches. But here are some extreme principles for living above the bland or the boring.

Stan Toler

If you're going to score, you gotta aim high!

"The quality of a man's life is in direct proportion to his commitment of excellence."

—Tom Landry

GOALS

I t was the last game of the tournament. Time was running out, and the score was tied. One of the players took the ball up the left side of the court, calling out the final play: a pick 'n' roll designed to put the ball in the hands of the team's best player. But when he set a pick for his teammate, no one switched, leaving a wide-open lane to the basket.

As the last seconds fell, the player ducked his head and drove the lane, shooting just in time. The ball slowly rose, then hit the bottom of the rim. As the players watched, they remembered the words of their coach: "To score, you gotta' aim high off the backboard." The player had all the right moves, but he missed because he didn't aim high enough.

That coach's advice works in every area of life. If you want to reach your goals, you have to aim high. Set goals that are reachable, but set them high enough that you have to stretch to reach them.

If you can dream it, you probably can do it.

Know where you're going.

"If you don't know where you're going, you're likely to end up someplace else."

—Yogi Berra

MISSION

O ne summer, two sisters decided to take a bike trip. They packed a few sandwiches, bottled water, and some Oreos in their backpacks, and off they went down a country road near their house. They peddled fast, laughed, and stopped at the creek to throw rocks in the water. Riding on a little bit farther, one rider suddenly stopped and asked, "By the way, where are we going?"

Her sister replied, "I don't know. I thought you knew!"

"Well, if we don't know where we're going, how will we know when we get there?" the rider responded.

Life is a lot like that. You'll never get where you want to go unless you decide where it is you *want* to go. What's your mission? College? Career? Family? Before you start the trip, think about your destination. Then think about going in the right direction and about the route you're going to take. And be sure to pack your backpack!

If you want to get somewhere, know where you're going.

You have to dig to discover.

"Even if you are on the right
track, you'll get run over
if you just sit there."

—Brent Hardesty

DISCOVERY

Archeology is a dirty job, but somebody has to do it. By the way, have you ever met an archeologist who found anything without digging to find it? The great archeological discoveries didn't just fall out of the sky. Someone dug them up. They discovered where the hidden treasures were and then committed themselves to uncovering them. Just think, without digging, King Tut's tomb would just be another basement apartment! The archeologists who found the tomb made their outstanding discovery only after a diligent search.

You can make a diligent search of your life. There are things about you that will never be discovered until you start digging. For example, you may have hidden talents and abilities. You may have the talent to be a great musician, the ability to be a best-selling author, or the interest and skills to be a renowned computer programmer. Perhaps you have those talents and don't know it. Start searching by trying new things, practicing the things you can do, and being open to using your abilities.

The talents you discover may be your own.

Give God
your best.

"Do the best you can with what
you have, wherever you are!"

—Adam Toler

EFFORT

Think about the teachers whom you really like or that coach whom you really respect. You'd do almost anything to please them. You work hard for them, complete all of your homework, and turn it in on time. Often, you stay after practice to shoot free throws. You give those individuals your best because of your devotion to them. These teachers get your best because you believe in the things that they believe are important.

Personal faith is your devotion to God. He also wants your very best effort. Imagine it. The Creator of the universe wants a relationship with you—a relationship of faith, hope, peace, and forgiveness. Your relationship with Him includes giving Him your very best. The awesome thing is, He wants to give His very best to you.

Being devoted to Him includes believing not only in Him; it also means believing in the things that are important to Him—His world, the people whom He loves, truth, and character.

Before you could even count, you could count on Him!

Give by the bag-loads.

"We make a living by what
we get; we make a life
by what we give."

Winston Churchill

GENEROSITY

Remember the pair of pants in your closet that you haven't worn in two years or the shirt that is still nice but just hasn't been in your regular rotation of clothes? Here's an idea: take a bag to your closet and fill it with all the clothes you don't wear anymore—even throw in a shirt you really like—and take it down to the local Goodwill or Salvation Army store. Giving is a rewarding experience.

Rewards are everywhere these days. You fly a particular airline, and you get so many free air miles in return. Purchase four CDs, and you get one free. Giving offers rewards as well. What you give is what you get. The first reward goes to the people who receive your gift. They are rewarded by your interest in them and your compassion for their need. The second reward goes to you. When you commit a random act of unselfishness, it simply makes you feel good inside.

Be generous with others. It's worth the investment.

Be nice on purpose.

"Do what you can to show
you care about other people,
and you will make our
world a better place."

—Rosalynn Carter

KINDNESS

Have you ever wanted to do something nice for someone? Why not just do it? Make an effort to be nice to people in small and big ways. Maybe you could walk around your neighborhood and pick up trash. Perhaps you could let your younger brother or sister hang out with you when you're around your friends. Be nice to others. Smile and show people that you care about them even though you don't know them.

Then just step back and watch. It's a riot! Unexpected kindness catches people off guard. If you're being paid to be nice, that's only half fun. But when you're nice for free, that's major fun! Whether you're working behind the fast-food counter, bagging groceries in a supermarket, waiting on customers in a retail store, or receiving any of these services, throw in an act of kindness. Give an encouraging word. Give a compliment. Ask people how they are feeling.

Go the extra mile, and you'll go a long way.

Listen and learn.

"Talk is cheap because supply exceeds demand."

—Anonymous

LISTENING

Have you ever tried to talk with a friend who just wouldn't be quiet? Every time you tried to put your "nickel's worth" in, he or she just kept talking, and rambling, and going on, and on, and on. If you've ever felt that way about a friend, look into your own life. Do you ramble? Are you a good listener?

In a day of cell phones, Palm Pilots, and e-mail, there's just too much output. Sometimes you need a little input. Sometimes you simply need to be quiet and listen. Listen to your friends. Listen to a family member. Listen to yourself. Listen to God. Remember to unplug and just listen.

Listening is step one in learning. You learn by listening to others. Their life experiences can really help you. Why not learn from their triumphs and tragedies? Why make their mistakes? Listen for the advice that will help you avoid some pain. All you need is an open mind and a closed mouth.

Quiet—learning in progress.

Stay on the "grow."

"It's what you learn after you know it all that counts."

—Coach John Wooden

GROWING

After you reach a certain age, do you stop eating? Like, once you're fifty, do you still have to eat? Of course you do. You have to eat every day to be truly healthy. Your body needs a constant intake of nutrients, minerals, and sugar for growth. Weird diets and quick-fix weight-loss schemes are dangerous because they may short-circuit your growth— and ruin your health in the process.

Your mind also needs a constant intake of knowledge. You're never too young or too old to learn. But learning isn't caught like a cold. It's done on purpose. You learn by putting stuff into your mind. Positive stuff has a positive effect. Guess what? Negative stuff has a negative effect. Your "intake choices" make a difference in your daily attitude.

How about spiritual growth? You not only need to "feed your *face*"; you also need to "feed your *faith*." Taking time for Bible reading and prayer is like stopping for lunch. Both activities have a positive and powerful effect.

Way to "grow"!

Learn to enjoy daily routines.

"I am only one, but still I am one. I cannot do everything, but still I can do something. And because I cannot do everything, I will not refuse to do the something I can do."

—Edward Everett Hale

ROUTINE

Laying bricks isn't the most exciting work in the world. It's tough work, and it requires time and skill. Sometimes it's plain boring—one brick after another, measure, place the brick, add the cement, and scrape off the surplus. It's a continual process. But seeing the beautiful house or majestic cathedral as a finished product makes it all worthwhile.

Everyday life is a lot like laying bricks—one chore after another, routine. Hear the alarm clock. Try to wake up. Shower. Brush your teeth. Comb your hair. Choose your wardrobe. Go to the same school. Go to the same job. Do the same thing all day. Come home. Get enough rest to do the same thing tomorrow. The routine things may be the toughest.

Turning really routine stuff into really cool stuff begins in your mind with thoughts like these: "I'm alive!" "I can make an impact on the world today!" "I can change someone's life with a word or an action!"

Are you bricklaying? Find meaning in the bricks. You're building a cathedral that will stand forever.

Make truth a priority.

"Our society finds Truth too strong a medicine to digest undiluted. In its purest form Truth is not a polite tap on the shoulder; it is a howling reproach. What Moses brought down from Mount Sinai were not the Ten Suggestions . . . they are commandments."

—Ted Koppel

HONESTY

Our first president, George Washington, is supposed to have said, "I cannot tell a lie," when he had to 'fess up to his father about chopping down the cherry tree. "I cannot tell a lie" doesn't mean he wasn't capable of lying. It simply means that he made some character choices. "I cannot" means "I will not." Today that story seems a bit old-fashioned and funny. Can't you just picture this little boy in a white wig hacking down a tree? Truth is, the message of the story is as fresh now as it was then.

Our founding father taught us a very important lesson: We must always be truthful, even when telling the truth seems out of style or if it will cost us something. Honesty is the best policy. Lying may get you out of a tight situation now, but it will just plain *get you* later. It's like deleting a harmful e-mail. It's gone from the screen, but it's still on your hard drive.

Watch out for *truth* decay!

Anticipate a surprise!

"'For I know the plans I have
for you,' declares the Lord,
'plans to prosper you and not to
harm you, plans to give you
hope and a future.'"

—Jeremiah 29:11

ANTICIPATION

While Billy was walking past his older brother's room, he heard some strange noises. He got up really close to the door and pressed his ear against the wood. It sounded like his brother was either doing push-ups under his bed or building the Eiffel Tower! Instead of knocking, Billy just opened the door and walked into the room. His brother tried to jump in his way and cover his eyes, but it was too late. Billy saw the pieces of a new bike lying on the floor. His brother was putting it together so his parents could give it to Billy at his birthday party the next day. Billy ruined the surprise.

Be careful not to ruin your surprises. "Nothing good ever happens to me." "I never get a break." "There's no way I can 'ace' that exam."

Anticipate a surprise. It could be that somebody's "building a bike" for you. Believe the best, even in the worst situations. Positive thoughts often bring positive results.

Keep a surprise in your heart. You never know when you might need it.

Say "I'm sorry" when you're wrong.

"When you're wrong, admit it, and when you're right, shut up!"

—Anonymous

OPENNESS

Have you ever heard the expression "Some things are better left unsaid"?

That doesn't always work. For example, as a small child, did you ever do something that you knew was wrong? Maybe you were sorry for doing it but didn't know how to tell your parents, so you tried to avoid them. Maybe you ran to your room and hid in the closet.

After twenty minutes or so, you realized that no matter how long you hid, you would still have to face your parents. So you walked slowly to the living room and mumbled, "I'm sorry." If you had said it right away, you'd have saved twenty minutes of worrying in that closet!

It's always better to say, "I'm sorry," than to just think it. Telling someone you're sorry for your words or actions brings the potential for healing to them, and it also brings closure to you. Telling your family or friends about your feelings is risky, but it's worth it.

Better to be *said* than sorry!

Be choosy about your friends.

"You will never soar with the eagles if you spend your time running around with a bunch of turkeys."

—Carl Summer

SELECTION

Apple farmers know how delicious a bushel of apples can be. They also know how much damage one little worm can do to that bushel of apples. They know that the tiny worm doesn't take a bite out of every apple in the bushel; it only has to find one. If an apple looks like someone's been chewing on it, the farmer throws it out. By doing so, he gets rid of the bad apple along with the "chewer" (the worm).

Know any worms?

Just like a worm, one person with bad habits or one who is a bad influence can ruin a whole group of friends. And just like the worm, he or she works on one person at a time until that person, too, becomes a "bad apple."

Be choosy about your friends. Do the people you hang out with reflect the best things about you? Do they represent your values? Do you have to stoop to be like them, or do they have to rise to be like you?

Don't hang out with worms.

Practice the attitude of gratitude.

"The deepest principle of human nature is the craving to be appreciated."

—William James

GRATITUDE

Sometimes you receive things that are undeserved. For instance, the light turns green at just the right moment. Maybe the grade on the test is so much better than you thought it was going to be that you just about pass out! Sometimes, right out of the blue, that certain someone suddenly notices you. Most of us acquire things that we don't deserve, and with them comes the responsibility of being grateful.

Do good things just happen, or do they happen because someone has the power to bring them into your life? You guessed it! Someone does. God brings goodness into your life. He is the source of every turn for the better. He is the sunshine behind every cloud. When you get ready to be grateful for the good things, then you're ready to thank God.

How's your gratitude machine? Is it in good working order? Is there any rust on it? Crank it up. Keep it in good condition.

Don't just "Thank Goodness!" Thank God.

Ask God to forgive you.

"I will not stifle the efforts of the
Holy Spirit to make a great
Christian out of me."

—Stan Toler

WEDGES

Have you ever seen anyone cut a tree down the old-fashioned way—with an ax and a wedge? The cutter chops a slice in the side of the tree and then uses an ax or a sledgehammer to drive a wedge shaped like the head of the ax farther into the tree. The pressure of the wedge causes a weakness and separation in the tree, making it easier to chop it down.

Weakness and separation can happen in your relationship with God too. An unconfessed sin, an attitude of rebellion against His will, or an unforgiving spirit toward someone who did you wrong is like a wedge between God and you. It weakens your fellowship with Him. It causes a break in the lines of communication toward Heaven. Spiritual wedges make you vulnerable to the attacks of your spiritual enemy.

The longer the wedge is left there, the more that separation weakens your relationship with God. Get rid of it quickly. Ask God to forgive you for the things that separate you from Him.

Get rid of the wedges!

Work hard.

"It has been my observation
that most people get
ahead during the time
that others waste."

—Henry Ford

DEPENDABILITY

Judy's dad worked in a local factory. The work was demanding, but her father didn't go home and lie on the couch after work. Since he was a single parent, he made sure the house was in order: the dishes were done, things were picked up, and so on. And after that, he would go outside and mow the lawn. He knew others in the home were depending on him. He knew the house would not take care of itself and, though he was tired, he had a responsibility.

Whether you're a volunteer or a paid worker, remember, someone is depending on you. Your work makes a difference. When you work in a responsible manner, you create a good impression and help lighten someone else's load.

Be a dependable worker. Do what your supervisor asks you to do. Arrive on time. Finish your work. Be neat and clean. Smile. Go the extra mile.

If you want to be a good worker, give it your best effort!

Honor your parents.

"All that I am or hope to be I
owe to my mother."

—Abraham Lincoln

RESPECT

If you're familiar with the Ten Commandments, you know the expression "Honor your father and mother." Of course, it's the commandment that usually comes up when there is a parent-teen discussion. Why not think about the commandment in a different light? Did you know that it's a commandment that comes with a payoff? The Bible says to honor your parents so that "it may go well with you and that you may enjoy long life on earth."

Honoring your parents doesn't mean bowing down to them when they walk through the door. Honoring your parents is an inward thing. It means to respect their values. It also means living by their rules—not out of duty, but out of your love for them.

Honoring your parents means looking out for their welfare. Always remember, love is a two-way commitment. When they love you enough to provide for your protection, you acknowledge and appreciate their support in return.

Respect is voluntary, not forced. Honor your parents on purpose.

Focus on the good in everyone.

"Every child born into the
world is a new thought
of God, an ever-fresh
and radiant possibility."

—Kate Douglas Wiggins

OUTLOOK

An ancient proverb says, "Focusing on the gloom and doom makes even your bones tired." It's hard to focus on the positive when you feel like slumping around in your own little world of doom. Often it's just as hard to see the positive in other people, but if you focus on the negative, it eats away at your very core. It makes your bones tired.

Look for the good in others. Every person has at least one good characteristic. Why not stretch to find it? It's there. God created human life, and He doesn't do inferior work. When you discover that good quality in a person, focus on it. Think about the good instead of the bad.

Look at life's circumstances in the same manner. Develop a healthy outlook. Some look at the sky and see the clouds. Determine to look for the sunbeams. A positive outlook chases the blues away. It makes you strong. It influences and encourages the naysayers as well.

Grade life on the curve!

Give love a chance.

"There is no fear in love.
But perfect love drives out
fear, because fear has to
do with punishment."

—1 John 4:18

CARING

Kyle was a loner. When he moved with his parents and attended a new school, he kept to himself. He never talked to anyone. He never let anyone get close to him. He was afraid to love. He didn't let his feelings for others show out of fear that they wouldn't feel the same way. Parents, friends, classmates, coworkers—it didn't matter. Everyone was kept at a distance.

At times, Kyle saw people who were in real need and wanted to reach out to them. He wanted to show his love and concern for them. But he didn't want to take a chance on showing his true feelings. He didn't understand that loving others is a risk worth taking. Love openly expresses itself, even if it's being misunderstood or rejected.

Give love a chance. Be open with others about your feelings. Your heart and your head will tell you when and how, but let it happen. Show someone you care.

If you keep your feelings bottled up too long, they might spoil.

Practice abstinence.

"True love waits!"

—Josh McDowell

VALUES

Everyone has beliefs or values that determine how he or she will act or react in a given situation. Whether they are spiritual, moral, financial, or political, you, too, have values that affect your behavior. There are some things you are willing to do and some things you won't do simply because of what you believe.

Television, magazine, and billboard ads try to influence your beliefs. For instance, some challenge you to wait until you are married before you have a sexual relationship. "I'm worth it," the ad slogan reminds you. That's the same as saying, "I have some beliefs about my self-worth that will determine my behavior."

Abstinence may not be the most popular belief. But it's a good one—and a practical one. Just think of all the things you have to worry about now. Do you really want to carry all the baggage that comes with growing up too fast?

Put your value system to work. Say, "I'm too valuable to do anything contrary to my beliefs."

Your commitment to abstinence may influence someone else just when he or she is making decisions about his or her own behavior.

Values are valuable.

Aim to please God, not others.

"Dear God,
Your will,
nothing more,
nothing less,
nothing else."

—A. B. Simpson

FOCUS

When you're at the mall and you discover some awesome shoes, what happens when you show them to your friends? There will be those who think the shoes are the best they've seen. There will be some who are jealous. They'll discourage you in hopes of buying the same pair for themselves later. Some will laugh so hard they'll fall down. That will be the moment when you realize you can't make everyone happy.

Trying to please people can be a frustrating and painful experience. About the time you think you've pleased one person, another one comes along. Now your attention is diverted. You stop trying to earn the favor of the first person in order to influence the second. If you ride that cycle, you'll end up crashing.

The Bible says to love God with all your heart—to focus your attention on Him. Focusing on God means trying to please Him in your attitudes and actions. And the cool thing is, when you focus on God, your relationships with others will get better.

Remember, God first and others next.

Find the funny in everyday life.

"A great man is he who does not lose his child's heart."

—Mencius

HUMOR

Linda took a shortcut through her backyard one fall afternoon. She was deep in thought when she accidentally stepped on the rake her brother had forgotten to put away. The handle of the rake flew up and hit her right on the nose. Soon her eyes and nose were black and blue.

Linda had a choice to make. Either she could be upset about the incident, or she could decide to have a good laugh. She decided to laugh. At school the next day, she told her friends in the cafeteria about the rake. As she went into the funny details of stepping on the rake, her friends laughed loudly. It was a fun break for all of them in the midst of an otherwise ordinary day.

Let's face it. Life has its silly moments, and many of them will happen to you. Instead of being embarrassed about them, why not turn them into a good story and brighten up someone's day?

Go for the funny.

Think before you jump to conclusions.

"There are many things in life that will catch your eye, but only a few will catch your heart. Pursue these!"

—George W. Bush

JUDGING

Think before you leap," the saying goes. That's pretty good advice in any situation. But it's especially good advice when you encounter other teens' questionable behavior. Before you start pronouncing judgment like Judge Judy, be sure you have all the facts. There may be a perfectly good explanation for the words or actions you have just witnessed.

Truly, it comes down to believing the best about people. The easy route is to believe the worst about an individual. All you have to do is swim downstream with the rest of your feathered friends who are ducking their responsibility by not looking at the facts.

Believing the best also leads to saying the best. It's better to hold that thought rather than turning it into a lethal weapon. Spreading rumors doesn't take much strength, but it can have a deadly force. With a word or two, you can kill someone's reputation and cause him or her heavy-duty pain.

So if you don't know the facts, believe the best first and the worst last.

Don't borrow tomorrow's troubles.

"God will never lead you where
His grace cannot keep you."

—L. B. Hicks

WORRY

Midnight is an interesting time of the day. At twelve o'clock, today's problems become yesterday's problems. "Live one day at a time" is perhaps the best advice you'll ever hear. And as long as you're going to live one day at a time, you might as well choose today. You can't do much about yesterday, and you certainly can't do anything about tomorrow until it gets here. Worrying about yesterday is a waste of time. It's better to focus on meeting the challenges of today.

Worrying about tomorrow drains life's energy. Borrowing tomorrow's trouble saps your strength. In some cases, it has even caused physical or mental illness.

Too much worry shows a lack of faith in God. Remember, God is eternal. He existed before time and will exist after time on earth is done. God knows as much about your tomorrow as He does about your today. You can trust Him for the unknown, because it's well known to Him.

Seize the day! Tomorrow's troubles may turn into tomorrow's triumphs.

If you borrowed it, return it.

"As you prove your trustworthiness in smaller matters, more of the world's valuable resources will become available to you."

—Stan Toler

TRUSTWORTHINESS

Chris loved to take things apart and put them back together. To do that, he often needed tools from his father's toolbox. The problem was, most of the time he forgot to put them back! So, when Chris's dad needed his tools for a project, he usually had to search for them. That not only slowed the work on Dad's project, it also caused problems in their relationship.

Dad didn't mind his son borrowing the tools, but he tried to stress the importance of returning things when you borrow them. Whether you're borrowing tools, sports equipment, clothing, or anything else, you should make it a point to return the items on time.

That's a great habit for two reasons. First, it makes it easier on the people whose stuff you borrowed. They won't have to hunt you down to find the missing items. Second, it teaches you how to be trustworthy. Your faithfulness here will also help you in other areas. Plus, you're developing a good habit, and good habits lead to good character.

Many happy returns!

Make time for your family.

"At the very core of modern civilization, the motor of the world is the family. All that is good, bad, or indifferent in every society, old and new, flows out of the health and effectiveness, or lack thereof, of the family."

—Joe Batten

PRIORITIES

Have you ever watched a litter of kittens? They explore their surroundings together. They play with each other. They fuss and fight. They try to be first in line at the "cafeteria." But after a while, they usually end up cuddling together for warmth or rest. Their security is in their relationship to each other.

Their interaction actually strengthens them. Their muscles are being trained in their playing with each other. Their senses are being sharpened as they look out for each other. Their emotions are being developed by their dependence on the others. Family is a priority to the kittens.

You're living in a very busy time right now. You're exploring your world—homework, after-school practices, recitals, study groups, part-time jobs—but it would be a good idea to follow the example of the kittens and make your family relationships a priority.

Make some time for family. Feel the warmth of the huddle. Let them be a source of strengthening. Settle any differences with them for the sake of your own security.

Remember, in life, it's the "litter" things that count!

Make a daily appointment with God.

"I have so much to do today
that I shall spend the first
three hours in prayer."

—Martin Luther

DEVOTION

When you want to hang out with your friends, you don't just leave it up to chance. You set up a specific time and place to meet them. Then you look forward to the meeting. You know you'll have some important stuff to talk about. You'll make some plans. You may even use your meeting time to tell them how you feel about them—to let them know about your devotion to them.

A meeting with God is like that—and more. Your daily appointment with God is a time for talking with Him, a time for sharing what's on your heart, and a time for expressing your devotion to Him.

While God is not limited to a scale of time, we are. To make sure that we meet with Him each day, we should make an appointment. That doesn't limit our experience with God. We can meet with Him anytime and anywhere, but setting a specific time to talk with Him in prayer and to read His Word helps us make it a regular occurrence.

Be devoted to your devotions.

Visit your local library.

"Man's mind, once stretched by a new idea, never regains its original dimensions."

—Oliver Wendell Holmes

IMPROVEMENT

What if there were a building where you could go to find the secrets of emotional, spiritual, physical, and mental improvement? There is! It's the public library.

Your local library is full of great books, magazines, newspapers, and audiovisual resources. You don't have to sign up for some expensive, mail-order, self-improvement program. All you have to do is spend some free time at the library.

Self-improvement is a key to your personal growth. If you want to "move up the ladder," you need to lean it against the local library. Your librarian will take you to just the right section, or help you find the computerized source, to help you stay a step ahead of the crowd.

Learn about the past in great history books. The triumphs and tragedies of the past will help you learn how to face the future. Learn about the present. Find out about your world. Keep a newspaper in one hand and a good book on current events in the other.

There are some good books at the library. Check it out!

Give someone a helping hand.

"You can hardly become
greedy or selfish when you
are busily sharing what
you have with others."

—Steve Weber

HELPFULNESS

If you saw an elderly lady struggling to get her groceries into her car, what would you do? You'd help her, of course. Making someone's burden a little lighter by putting some of it on yourself is one of the most rewarding experiences in life. The things you do for free usually turn out to be the most valuable. They'll stay with you a lot longer than the things you are paid to do.

Helpfulness is a habit that is developed, just like in-line skating or riding a motorcycle. Start small. Offer your place in line to the person behind you. Pick up that gum wrapper in the aisle at the store. Take a turn doing the supper dishes.

Then move up a notch. Offer to baby-sit for a friend or relative. Paint the house of a shut-in. Take a shift working in the kitchen at a homeless shelter. Do maintenance work on the auto of a single mom. Volunteer to be a camp counselor.

If you hear the word "Help!" answer the call.

Dream big dreams.

"Start by doing what's
necessary, then what's possible,
and suddenly you are doing
the impossible."

—St. Francis of Assisi

ATTITUDE

Champions usually don't win their titles by accident. They plan for them. They always begin the competition with just that one goal in mind: winning. Even if the statistics are against them, they still believe they can overcome.

Champions win big because they dream big. In one sense, winning begins in your mind. If you can see yourself crossing the goal, you have a great incentive for running the race. Your attitude makes all the difference.

Take that attitude into the other areas of your life as well. When you think of your future, think big. Why settle for being a parking lot attendant at the medical clinic if you have the potential for being one of the physicians? Never settle for second best. Aim to study, work, or play at your highest level of achievement.

Here's a good principle: Attitude plus effort equals accomplishment. If you can see it in your mind, you're on the way to making it a reality. If you want some big realities, then you'd better do some big dreaming.

You've gotta believe it in order to see it!

Manage your minutes.

"Real time management is self-management."

—Stan Toler

EFFICIENCY

Everyone has the same 1,440 minutes to work with each day—no more and no fewer. The management of those minutes is what's important. They fly by more swiftly than an eagle. You sit down to watch a few minutes of television, and suddenly an hour or two passes. The same thing happens when you play computer games. Minutes turn into hours before you know it.

Learning how to efficiently manage your time is one of the most important skills you will ever develop. Time must be controlled, or it will control you. Use a daily planner or a handheld computer to map out your minutes.

Spend some of your minutes in planning. What goals do you want to reach today? Make a list. Then learn how exciting it is to cross an activity off your list after you've accomplished it. Spend some of your time in quiet reflection. Take the time to reflect on your day, and include some time for prayer and Bible study.

Learn to conquer your minutes, and you'll have hours to spare.

Join a church youth group.

"Let us not give up meeting together, as some are in the habit of doing, but let us encourage one another— and all the more as you see the Day approaching."

—Hebrews 10:25

FELLOWSHIP

People need other people. That's just the way we're made. We have this inner longing for friendships. But our friendships can be a negative influence on our lives as well as a positive one. A common faith, and its accompanying values, is an important factor in building positive relationships.

In almost every town, there is a group of people your age that meets in association with a local church to share common beliefs. That kind of friendship is called fellowship. These meetings are usually very positive and are all about building God-centered relationships and friendships.

A church youth group is designed to offer a cool place to hang out and be surrounded by people who have a common relationship with God.

If you want to add a great dimension to your friendships, look for a church with an active youth group, and then get involved. How do you find one? Ask your friends. Look for the church ads in your newspaper. Ask a family member who attends church.

You need the group, and the group needs you!

Overcome failure with faith.

"You can't make footprints on the sands of time sitting down. Take a step of faith!"

—Jerry Brecheisen

TRUST

What is faith? Faith is an inner belief, or trust, in something or someone. It's not something you can see or touch. Often, you believe in something even though you can't fully understand it. For example, if you drive a car, you put a key into the ignition, and you trust that by turning the key you will start the engine. You also believe that turning the key will start a chain of events that will take you from where you are now to where you want to go.

Have you ever heard of people who lost faith in something or someone? They stopped believing because they encountered setbacks in their lives. Actually, setbacks are a good place to put faith into action. A champion figure skater doesn't quit a routine because of a fall. He or she gets up from the ice, continues the routine, and then uses the incident as a learning point. The skater overcomes the setback by believing that he or she will do better the next time.

Can you overcome your setbacks? You'd better believe it!

Stop and smell the popcorn.

"God has given me this day to use as I will. I can waste it, or use it for good, but what I do today is important because I am exchanging a day of my life for it."

—Heartsell Wilson

RELAXATION

You live in an over-stimulated society. You rush from school to practice, to a job, to homework, and then to the mall for a soft drink—all in the same afternoon. All of the things you're involved in may be great, but sometimes you just need to push the "pause" button. You need to stop and smell the popcorn. You need to chill out once in a while.

Your body needs it. Your teen years are times of accelerated growth. Your body is in high gear, and it's going through tremendous changes. Once in a while you need to stop long enough for your legs to keep up with your arms! Times of relaxation allow your cells to regroup and rest for the work ahead.

Your mind needs it too. Sometimes it's on overload. Homework, scripts, songs, plays, PIN numbers, cell phone numbers—you have a lot to think about. Sometimes you just need to stop thinking. Relax. Put your mind in neutral. It has a long trip ahead of it.

Enjoy your life; you only have one!

Control your temper.

"Raised voices lower esteem.

Hot tempers cool friendships.

Loose tongues stretch truth.

Swelled heads shrink influence.

Sharp words dull respect."

—William A. Ward

DISCIPLINE

With a "crack," the ball hit the baseball bat and went sailing into the air toward center field. It seemed like it almost left the earth's atmosphere. Freddie ran back as fast as he could and positioned himself right underneath it. The ball came down fast. Then it hit the tip of his glove and fell to the ground. Angry about his error, Freddie grabbed the ball and, out of frustration, turned and threw it as hard as he could. The ball went flying over the third baseman's head and rolled out into the parking lot. Because he acted quickly and was out of control, Freddie turned in the wrong direction. If he had controlled his anger, he would have known where he was throwing.

Life is filled with frustrating moments. How you discipline yourself to react to them makes all the difference. If you react quickly and out of anger, you will probably "throw in the wrong direction."

Take time to think about the problem, and think about your reaction. You'll make fewer errors.

Take a good look in the mirror.

"God has never made
a mistake!"

—Lon Woodrum

REFLECTION

One of the first things you do every morning is look in the mirror. That can be very scary, especially if you didn't get enough sleep the night before. But after you've showered, brushed your teeth, and done the first comb-through on your hair, the view in the mirror looks a little better. Later, after the final comb-through, or after the makeup is applied, the view improves.

Have you really looked in the mirror lately? What do you see? At first glance, you might see someone you're unhappy with. Your eyes are the wrong color. Your nose is too long or too short. You have a zit or two. But look again.

You are a valuable person in God's eyes. You have unique skills. You have the ability to make a difference in someone else's life. You are the right person for the job at hand. There are some adjustments you might need to make before you face the day, but the potential is there.

Put your "God glasses" on and take another look.

Never seek revenge.

"A bulldog can beat a skunk
any day, but it's usually
just not worth it!"

—S. M. Lockridge

SELFLESSNESS

W hat about my rights?" It's a common expression these days. Everyone is looking out for his or her own rights. Consequently, we seem to be living in a world where people look out only for themselves. And what happens when someone seems to violate our rights? Our natural instinct is to retaliate—word for word, action for action, hurt for hurt. It's payback time!

Jesus Christ was the most selfless person who ever lived on the earth. He taught us that there are times when we surrender our rights for the welfare of others. He surrendered His rights when He died on the cross. His death made it possible for you to be forgiven of your past and to be assured of a future filled with hope.

You can't control how other people will act toward you, but you can control how you will react toward them. Revenge is a selfish reaction. It also ends up hurting you more than it does anyone else. You end up with the guilt, bitterness, and anxiety.

Your rights could make a wrong.

Know what's happening in the world.

"You can't influence
a world with which
you are not familiar."

—Steve Weber

AWARENESS

One of the characteristics of successful people is that they are aware of their world. They use every opportunity to stay informed on current events. Business, political, social, religious, and sports news is available to them, and they take advantage of it. They know that an awareness of world events gives them an edge, whether it's in their personal decision-making or in their interaction with others.

To know what's going on in the world, you have to read. In just a few moments each day, you can become aware of what's happening in your world. For example, take a few minutes to look over the newspaper headlines. You don't have to read every word of every line in the newspaper to know what's in it. Scan the headlines. Read the first few sentences of each paragraph.

Another way to stay informed is to watch a television news program or to go to a news Web site. Look and listen for the main events.

It really doesn't take much effort to be "in the know."

Grab a book instead of the remote control.

"All leaders are readers.
The moment you stop reading,
you stop leading."

—Stan Toler

IMAGINATION

You've heard it a million times. There are posters up all over your school: "R-E-A-D." In some schools students even get free pizza for reading a certain number of books. Why do you think reading is so important? Is it a trick by the "powers that be" to make your life miserable and to take all the fun out of life?

Actually, your teachers are more concerned about your mind than they are about ruining a good time. They know that all of us have a tendency to take the easy way. They know that it's a lot easier for us to "veg out" with a soda, some tortilla chips, and the remote.

Did you know that your brain gets hungry just like your stomach? It needs nourishment and exercise just like the rest of your body. When you choose a book over the television once in a while, you jump-start your mind. You stir up your imagination. Getting your brain out of "neutral" and into "drive" keeps it alert and creative.

Give your mind a vacation from television. Grab a book instead of the remote.

Spend time with your grandparents.

"We should all have one person
who knows how to bless us
despite the evidence. . . .
Grandmother was
that person to me."

—Phillis Therony

WISDOM

*I*t's a different world, you think. *Nobody knows what I'm going through.* Sometimes, when you are young, you forget that people older than you have great wisdom. Sure, the world is a different place than it was fifty years ago. It really is a brand-new world. But life's struggles are the same. Education, career, relationships, faith—your grandparents faced those same issues. They have something that a college degree alone can't give. They have wisdom.

Wisdom combines learning with experience. Your grandparents understand your journey because they've been over some of those same roads. Spend some time with them. Learn about life. Find security in their love and admiration for you.

You don't have grandparents? Borrow some. There are people in your community who need someone just like you. What about that older couple in your church whose children are grown or whose grandchildren live out of town? Adopt them. Get to know them. You will be amazed at the stories you'll hear and the fun you'll have.

Let your grandparents teach you a thing or two about living.

Give someone a hug.

"Love is the one commodity we always have enough of. It's the only thing in life that is not diminished by being divided and shared."

—Linda Weber

AFFECTION

We were created with five senses, and one of those is the sense of touch. Imagine if you couldn't feel anything. You wouldn't know if a stove were hot or cold. You wouldn't know the fluffy softness of a puppy. You wouldn't know how comforting cotton pajamas feel on a lazy Saturday. But most importantly, you wouldn't be able to feel the touch of others. Touch is one way we show our love and affection for others.

Of course you know about "good touches" and "bad touches." But good touches are always in order—especially when it comes to members of your own family. Give someone a surprise hug. Show someone how much you care—spontaneously. Sometimes a hug needs an accompanying word, such as "I love you" or "I appreciate you." But most often, hugs are stand-alone signs of how you feel about someone.

Affection is a sign of life. It lets people know that your heart is still beating, that you're emotionally balanced, and that your relationships are important.

It's okay to be a "hug addict"!

Stop and look at a sunset.

"Life is not a matter of milestones, but of moments."

—Rose Fitzgerald Kennedy

BEAUTY

Every Saturday afternoon during the fall season, the church youth group got together and played football. Guy or girl, younger or older—everyone played. On one afternoon, it was getting late in the day, and the group was still playing. Suddenly, the quarterback on one team stopped playing and shouted, "Hey, everybody! Look at that sunset!" The players stood still, looking in awe at the golden brilliance of that fall sunset. For the moment, nothing else mattered but the beauty of the sun's last hurrah!

At first, it seemed crazy to stop the whole game for something that happens every day. But soon it made perfect sense. No other sunset would be just like this one. Its orange and gold hues were mixed especially for this day. Tomorrow's sunset would be different.

Don't miss today's sunset by getting too caught up in the game. Look around you and enjoy the beautiful things of God's creation. It will remind you of how silly it is to get so caught up with a hectic schedule that you forget what's really important.

Grab a lawn chair and watch the sun go down.

Look for a rainbow after the rain.

"The Lord is faithful to all his promises and loving toward all he has made."

Psalm 145:13

PROMISE

Gentle spring rains water the earth after winter and bring life back into nature. The smells are indescribable. Summer rainstorms seem to be more intense. They come quickly and drench the fields. Fall rains are cold and dreary. They seem sad and miserable.

Spring rains are like God's promise of newness after the sameness of winter. His promises are everywhere. The refreshing spring rain stops. Suddenly, beautiful colors shoot across the sky—a painted reminder that the rain won't last forever. After the Great Flood recorded in the Bible, God gave the assurance that the waters wouldn't destroy the earth again, and He sealed that promise with a rainbow. Each color was an added reminder of His goodness and love.

There will be some rain in your life—times when things just won't go as planned. Sickness, failures, and misunderstandings will come— some gently like spring rains and some more intense like summer rains. Some may even make you sad and miserable like winter rains.

But they won't last forever. That's a promise! God sealed it with a rainbow.

Volunteer your time.

"The time is always right
to do what is right."

—Martin Luther King Jr.

SERVICE

Think about it. You get a lot from your community: education, parks and recreation, police and fire services, transportation, social services. Wouldn't it be nice to give something back? Volunteering your time at an agency in your community is a way to do just that.

For example, hospitals are a great place to volunteer your time. They can be lonely places. Volunteering your time to work at the front desk or to transport patients to and from their rooms can be a way to add some kindness and cheer. Also, the hospital staff is probably overworked and would appreciate your help.

There are other agencies that need your help as well. Ask your school counselor or your pastor for some suggestions. You could volunteer to work in an office, be a tour guide, help clean up a local park, or make deliveries to the elderly. The list goes on.

You may even want to get some of your friends to work with you. Volunteering is contagious: Other teens will catch it from you.

Make a difference in your community. Give something back.

Plan ahead.

"Failing to plan = planning
to fail."

—Brent Hardesty

PREPARATION

If you want to go to your friend's house, you don't go out the front door and stand on the sidewalk, hoping for a brisk wind to take you there. You make some preparations. You think about the meeting time, transportation, what you're going to wear, and the route you're going to take. You plan ahead.

Here's a PLAN-AHEAD formula for your life:

P - Pray. Ask God for wisdom and direction.

L - List the things that need to be accomplished.

A - Acquire the information and resources you need to do the job.

N - Notice what others have done in similar situations.

A - Ask advice from some experts.

H - Heed your inner voice. Use caution if you feel uneasy.

E - Expect adversity and plan to overcome it.

A - Act decisively. Once you make your decision, go for it!

D - Do your best and leave the rest to God.

With a little preparation, you can work smarter and more effectively and worry less about what needs to be done.

Preparation before perspiration!

Read the directions.

"If you haven't got the time to do it right, when will you ever have the time to do it over?"

—Anonymous

INSTRUCTION

Been there, done that!" is a classic expression that says, "I've already experienced this." But what if you haven't? Then, a little advice is in order. Some instruction is needed. Have you ever tried to put something together without reading the directions first? Sometimes doing so can be painful. You put everything together, but there's one piece left over. Soon you make the awful discovery. That piece belongs right there—right in the middle of the project! Now your creation doesn't work right. The piece was necessary for its operation.

Life is a lot like that. Read the directions first. God has given awesome instructions in His Word, the Bible. Life is just too complicated to "play it by ear." Get all the help you can get. Read the directions and see how God has pieced it all together for you. If you try it by yourself, you get only what you can do. If you follow His instructions, you get what God can do.

Get out the "owner's manual" and start living.

Follow your heart.

"What lies behind us and
what lies before us are
small matters compared
to what lies within us."

—Ralph Waldo Emerson

CONVICTION

Have you ever been with your friends when they started doing something that you weren't comfortable with or just weren't sure about? You felt that strange feeling inside. What was it? It was your heart. Not your real, blood-pumping heart but your inner, conscience heart. When you feel that, it means you are probably doing something against your personal convictions—against your personal values.

It's good to listen to your heart in those situations. But to truly trust your own heart, you must align it with the truth—God's truth. God has given us two important things for moments like these. First, He has given us His written Word. You can check your behavior against the values that are written in the Bible. Second, He has given you His Spirit to live within you. As you have put your trust in Him, God has given you an inner warning system that will sound an alert when you cross over into "enemy territory."

If you don't stand for something, you'll take a fall!

Respect those who are in authority.

"Everyone must submit himself
to the governing authorities,
for there is no authority except
that which God has established.
The authorities that exist have
been established by God."

Romans 13:1

OBEDIENCE

Rebelling against authority seems to be the cool thing to do these days. You see people on television running from the police or throwing stones through store windows in one kind of protest or another. Maybe you've even seen some religious organizations rebelling against the laws of government.

It may seem to be the cool thing to do, but it's not the right thing. The Bible tells us to respect those who are in authority. That doesn't mean we have to agree with everything they say. It simply means we are to abide by what they say because they have the authority to say it.

We obey laws because it's right, not because it's convenient or popular. That takes personal discipline. It's easy to call police officers names or cover walls with graffiti in protest, but it takes discipline to do what is right instead of what's reactionary.

Obedience is a source of personal growth. Not only will it help you make adjustments in your home, it will help you in every other area of your life.

Obey or pay!

Clean up your language.

"Engage your brain before
opening your mouth!"

—Ed Jeffers

SPEECH

Have you ever seen a sink full of dirty dishes—dishes with chunks of dried food on them? They don't look good, and they smell even worse. Only flies like dirty dishes. For them, a sink full of dishes with garbage on them is like an "open" sign on a restaurant.

What's the solution for dirty dishes? Obviously, they need to be washed. A little soap, a little disinfectant, and that sink will be a better place. The flies will hate it, but people will love it.

Sometimes, speech can be as nasty as a sink full of dirty dishes. Think of the words that come out of your mouth. Or, think of the words that are ready to come out. Some of them may be just as nasty as dried food on a dinner plate. They foul up the place. They're not attractive to others, and they're not healthy. Watch your language. Think about those words before you let them out of your head.

Clean up your language, and your whole world will smell better.

Discover the importance of teamwork.

"Teamwork makes
the dream work!"

—S. Mark Hollingsworth

COOPERATION

Shelly had been shooting great the whole game. In the last seconds of her high school basketball game, the score was tied. She dribbled the ball up the court, focused quickly on the rim, and took a desperate shot with three opposing players all over her. The ball, thrown like a bullet, bounced off the backboard and into the hands of an opposing player. That player threw it quickly down the court to another player who put it into the basket with a winning lay-up.

Shelly was focused on her game, but she forgot about the importance of teamwork. The outcome would have been different if she had passed to her teammate who was in position under the goal.

Teamwork isn't for sports only. In almost every area of life, it's better to work in cooperation with others. Their experience and skills only add to yours. They may be in a better position to accomplish the task. Why not pass to them?

Don't do it alone. Pass to your friends, your family, or your coworkers. The game you save may be your own.

Write a letter to someone who has had an impact upon your life.

"None goes his way alone:
All that we send into the
lives of others comes back
into our own."

—Edwin Markham

APPRECIATION

Are you a better person because of someone you know? Why not let that person know how much you appreciate him or her? The person probably doesn't know how much he or she means to you. If someone has truly had an impact upon your life, write him or her a letter. In this day of e-mail and chat rooms, a letter might seem a bit old-fashioned or uncool. But when it comes to hand writing a note or letter, it truly is "the thought that counts."

That person to whom you are writing will be affected by the thought of how much effort went into the correspondence. Letter writing takes time and thought. The person who receives it will appreciate that.

Tell the person how grateful you are for having known him or her. Express your thanks for specific acts of kindness or help. Get out a pen and a piece of paper and let your thoughts fill the pages. Try to affect someone as he or she has affected you.

Someday your letter of appreciation may be "returned to sender."

Look people in the eye when you speak to them.

"The eye is a window into the soul."

—Debra White Smith

ATTENTION

Have you ever talked to someone who currently is in or has been in the military? If you have, did you notice that person's body language when he or she spoke to you? More than likely this person stood up straight, looked you in the eye, and generally showed an interest in what you had to say. His or her body language comes from a discipline acquired during training.

When you are talking with someone, be sure to focus your attention on him or her. Make eye contact, especially when you are being spoken to. This lets the person know that you are listening and that you respect his or her opinion.

Good eye contact says a lot about you. First, it speaks of your confidence in yourself. You are saying that you are on the same communication level—no matter what the other person's status may be. Second, looking someone in the eye says that you have confidence in that person. You are providing a communication link that will possibly be a great benefit to your relationship with him or her.

Try to see eye-to-eye with everyone.

Make it a habit to exercise regularly.

"Yesterday is a canceled check;
tomorrow is a promissory note;
today is the only cash
you have—take care
of your health today."

—Kay Lyons

FITNESS

You don't see too many adults out on the playground. But of course the playgrounds are full of kids running around, jumping over the teeter-totters, playing basketball, or swinging on the monkey bars. Maybe that's why you were in a lot better shape when you were younger. Think about how much time you spent exercising when you were a little kid. It's still a good thing to do.

You don't have to stop running and jumping now that you're older. In fact, exercise is beneficial no matter how old you are. Exercise will not only help you stay fit, but it's also a good way to relieve the stress of everyday life.

A good exercise routine starts in your mind. You have to decide to do it. Make some important choices about your health. Set some goals. Choose your methods. Then proceed with determination by establishing an unbreakable exercise habit. Determine to regain some of that energy you had as a kid.

Try on some exercise for a good fit.

Laugh a lot.

"Humor is the shock
absorbers of life."

—Barbara Johnson

LAUGHTER

Have you ever laughed until your stomach hurt? Or have you ever fallen out of your chair because you were laughing so hard? Why does it feel so good to laugh? It seems that something called "endorphins" are released every time you laugh—actually making you feel better. It's like nature's antidepressant.

Laughter is a universal language. It's so contagious that you can be in a country where you don't speak the native language and can get a whole bus load of people laughing, simply by laughing yourself.

Don't put a lid on your laughter. Laugh a lot. It's a great remedy for what ails you. Laughter can help you deal with disappointment or despair. Have you ever gone through bad times, turned on the television, and found yourself laughing at some comedian's routine? For the moment, your problems were lost in the laughter.

What would the world be like if everybody laughed more? Probably a lot different than it is right now. People who have learned to laugh can also be taught to love.

Laugh it up!

Learn from your older brothers or sisters.

"No human interaction has greater impact on our lives than our family experience."

—Armand Nicholi

IMITATION

Have you ever watched your older brothers or sisters while your parents were disciplining them? You probably learned something from their painful experiences! As a matter of fact, there's a lot to be learned by watching or listening to your siblings. No matter how much older they are, they have at least that much more experience.

They've experienced some difficulties that you could avoid simply by taking their advice. The very things that have been stumbling blocks to them may become stepping-stones to you. Imitate their best behavior.

Don't forget your younger siblings either. While you can teach them a lot, they might be able to teach you a few things as well. They are coming at life with a newer perspective.

Think of your siblings as friends, not just family. Keep the lines of communication open. Forgive quickly—not only for the sake of the family, but also for your own emotional well-being. Affirm what is right about them, and lovingly discourage their wrong.

If you make friends with your siblings now, you'll have fewer enemies later.

Show gratitude for your allowance.

"God gave you the gift of
86,400 seconds today. Have you
used one to say 'thank you'?"

—William A. Ward

ACKNOWLEDGMENT

Do you get an allowance from your parents? If so, what's your attitude toward your allowance? Do you expect it? Do you appreciate it? An allowance is not something that is yours by some birthright. It is given to you voluntarily. There may be some strings attached, but generally it comes from the kindness and concern of your parents.

An allowance is their way of teaching you responsibility. That's something you'll need plenty of when you enter the workforce. "A day's pay for a day's work" will be your employer's philosophy. It's great to learn about that now rather than later.

An allowance is also your parents' way of teaching you about money management. Your habits of spending or saving your allowance money will help you manage your money throughout your life, if you develop wise habits.

It also is their way of saying they trust you. It affirms their respect for your use of the money, and it shows their confidence in you.

Maybe it's a good time to acknowledge their generosity—to say "thank you." They don't have to give you an allowance. Be thankful that they want to.

Open a savings account.

"Make all you can.

Save all you can.

Give all you can."

—John Wesley

SAVING

Everywhere you look, you are being encouraged to spend. Television commercials, billboard messages, Internet advertisements, infomercials, magazine advertisements—they're all saying, "Spend your money here!" Learning how to spend wisely is very important to your future financial health, but so is learning how to save. Learning to put some of your hard-earned money into a savings account is a practice that will help you throughout your life.

Did you have a piggy bank when you were a kid? That bank taught you to make some sacrifices at the moment for the joy of breaking it open later and seeing how much you'd saved.

Well, when you get to the age you are now, it's time to take the pig to the bank. Instead of keeping your allowance or work money in a jar under your bed, it's time to open a savings account at the bank. It's a better way of tracking your spending, and it teaches you how to work with the financial institutions in your community to manage your money.

So, take "one little piggy to market."

Pay your bills on time.

"Character loans are
the best loans."

—John Baldwin, banker

DEBT

Debt is something you owe in return for goods or services you've received, like money you owe for the price of a bicycle or money you owe for having your hair cut. Sometimes that debt is paid off immediately—in cash. At other times, the debt or money you owe is paid back a little at a time.

How you handle your debts will determine your financial success or failure. An inevitable sign of growing up is the stack of bills that will soon show up in your mailbox. Many of them will come well over two weeks before they are due, and it will be very tempting to let them collect dust on your desk. But don't let them sit too long. Before you know it, the due date will pass and you will be making a late payment. Those late payments will be recorded on your credit report and will determine what you will be allowed to purchase later.

Always pay your bills when they are due, or even before.

Avoid credit card offers.

"Debt is emptying your future
to fill your present."

—Ron Blue

SPENDING

Maybe you've received one in the mail with your name on it. It's made out of plastic. It's millimeters thin. It has an attractive logo on the front. It hardly weighs a thing, but if you're not careful with it, it will be like a monster.

It's a credit card. It comes with a message: "BUY NOW!" It doesn't want you to think very long about whether you have enough money to pay the bill.

No, not all credit cards are dangerous. When they're in the hands of a responsible spender, they can be used effectively. But when they're used irresponsibly, they can do a lot of damage.

If you get one in the mail, or if you're tempted to sign up for one, it's a good time to have a talk with your parents about debt and about owing money that you can't repay. It's time to talk about alternatives like debit cards (cards used for purchasing that have specified limits backed up with the same amount of money in your bank account).

If you're going to use a credit card, use it wisely; don't let it use you.

Budget your money.

"A budget is nothing more than
a plan for spending money. . . .
It doesn't limit expenditures,
it defines them."

—Larry Burkett

BUDGETING

Have you ever seen your parents sit at the kitchen table and punch numbers into a calculator as they look at old receipts and bank statements? They aren't playing a game of Monopoly. They're probably working on their budget. A budget is a plan for using the money you earn—money that comes in—to pay the things that you owe—money that goes out. Your parents are tracking their income and their outgo to make sure there will be enough money left for the jelly on your peanut butter and jelly sandwiches!

Now is a good time for you to learn how to budget your money. You may not have a lot of income at this point, but whatever you have, list it. On the other side of the page, list the things you need to buy and the amount of money you owe to someone. Subtract your outgo from your income. How's the balance? That's the key to good budgeting.

Learn to live within your budget by making sure your outgo doesn't exceed your income.

Watch your spending.

"If your outgo exceeds your income, then your upkeep will be your downfall."

—William Aaron Toler, West Virginia coal miner

CHOICES

Some checkbooks look like they have revolving doors on them. Money goes in but immediately comes back out. Just because you have money in the bank—or some other form of savings—it doesn't mean you have to spend it. Careless and constant spending is a dangerous habit. Watch your spending like an eagle watches a rabbit sandwich. Your financial success depends on it. Constant spending will leave you without any reserves—and you never know when you'll need a little extra.

Almost every day of your life, you will be asked to make a money choice. Advertisers will want you to choose their products. But remember, they have one goal in mind: They want you to give up your money. The more you spend, the better off they are.

You don't have to spend your money. You can choose to save some of it. You can choose to be selective in what you purchase—not always choosing the most expensive, for instance.

So instead of a revolving-door checkbook, get one that actually shuts.

Ask God to heal your hurts.

"Don't rehearse your hurts,
nurse your hurts, or curse your
hurts. Give them to God!"

—Oral Roberts

HEALING

Maybe you've had the same family doctor since the time you were born. If so, he or she probably knows your physical condition even better than you know it yourself.

But no matter how long you've been associated with your family physician, God knows you better. He created you. He knows every cell, every bone, every muscle, and every inch of skin. He even knows about your hurts before you begin hurting.

Of course, not all of your hurts are obvious. Some are hidden so deep that even your best friend doesn't know about them. But God does. He sees the hidden things of your life. He cares about you more than anyone on earth does.

And, just as you would make an appointment with your doctor for help with a physical hurt, you can go to God with your inner hurts. Anger, loneliness, bitterness, rejection—He knows about them. He wants to give you His healing.

Ask Him. Not only can He heal you physically, but He can also heal you emotionally and spiritually. And besides, He even makes house calls.

Don't take all of the shortcuts.

"Too much is at stake to take shortcuts, hope for the best, or assume someone else will do a good job."

—Linda Weber

LOYALTY

In a marathon race, if you take a shortcut to get ahead of the pack, you are immediately disqualified. When a track is clearly marked out, no shortcut will do.

In life, there are a lot of shortcuts you may take. But not all of them are good for you—and some will even disqualify you. For example, if you've been given a job to do, do it the way your employer asked. Even if you've found a shortcut for accomplishing the task, it would be better for you to do it the boss's way than your way.

Throughout your life, you'll be tempted to take the easy way out—shave a little effort here; give 90 percent instead of 100 percent; fudge the statistics a little; leave work a few minutes early. But in the long run, you'll be the loser. You can probably pull the wool over your supervisor's eyes temporarily, but overall the odds are on his or her side.

Do what you've been asked—and more. Loyalty pays.

Establish regular study habits.

"I have found that the harder I work, the luckier I seem to be!"

—Norman Vincent Peale

STUDY

Has your closet ever been so full that you had to just start cramming things in to make everything fit? What usually happens when you open the door the next day? Everything falls out, right? Or have you ever jammed so many clothes into a drawer that you couldn't get it shut?

Imagine that your brain is a drawer or closet. Cramming a bunch of facts into it the night before a big exam may get you a passing grade once in a while—but usually everything falls out, even before you get to the classroom.

If you want to do well on your tests, establish a study routine. Choose a time and place where you regularly open the books. Studying regularly is a lot better than studying frantically. Store facts in your brain a little at a time. It's just like storing information in files on the hard drive of your computer. If you store them properly, they're easier to find later.

If you put too much on your mind's hard drive, you're in for a crash.

Read the Bible regularly.

"How can a young man keep his way pure? By living according to your word."

—King David (Psalm 119:9)

ILLUMINATION

It's there in the back of your desk drawer. You kept it because of what it says and because of the one who sent it to you. It's a very special letter.

In it, the writer told you how much he or she cared about you, and how your relationship could even be improved. The advice is so good, it will be just as valuable tomorrow as it is today. That's why you saved it in that special place.

God wrote you a letter—the Bible. In fact, since the Bible is divided into sixty-six different "books," it is like a stack of letters. Each one is special. And each was written with you in mind, so it means more to you every time you read it.

Read it for illumination. Understanding its message will guide you in all areas of your life. It's your "owner's manual."

Read it for inspiration. Hear God's words of affirmation and concern for you by reading its pages. It's filled with God's "love letters" to you.

When all else fails, read God's directions.

Write out your life goals.

"You will never leave where you
are behind until you decide
where you would rather be."

—Melvin Maxwell

VISION

In soccer, seeing the goal isn't that difficult for the players. Why? It's not difficult because the goal is clearly visible from anywhere on the field. It would be impossible for anyone to score if he or she didn't know where the goal was.

It's the same in other areas of your life. If you have clearly marked goals, it will be easier for you to make progress. You usually achieve the things that you first "see" in your mind. So your progress is a result of your "vision."

What's your vision for life? Try writing down some of your goals and keeping them in a place where you can review them periodically. Where do you want to be four years from now? Two years from now? Next year? How about making some practical goals for your education, your career, or your finances? It's a great habit, and it's one that will help you later on.

You don't reach your goals accidentally. Pray about them, think about them, list them, and then head for them!

Communicate your feelings to your parents.

"You will never understand your parents love and concern for you until you are one."

—Linda Toler

SHARING

It's an interesting paradox. Those who probably care the most about how you feel are usually among the last to know your inner feelings. Maybe it goes with the territory. The tremendous changes that are happening in your mind and your body are both confusing and very private. Or maybe it's just an assumption. You assume that people who are always around you should know how you feel without your having to spell it out.

So you stay unplugged. You hide your joys and your hurts like a basset hound with a neighbor dog's bone. And you dig them up only when you want to—and show them only to your best friend. But bones have a way of getting excavated (like a dinosaur skeleton). Hidden feelings may surface in ways that are both personally painful and painful to those you love most.

How about sharing with your parents what you are feeling? Who knows? They might even open up and tell you how *they're* feeling! Before you know it, you could have a real communication thing going.

Dare to share your heart!

Be on time.

"People count the faults of those who keep them waiting."

—French Proverb

PROMPTNESS

Winners have certain characteristics. Promptness is one of them. Highly successful people make it a habit to be on time for their appointments. Being on time shows your interest in the meeting, and it shows that you care about the person you are meeting with. Tardiness is actually a form of selfishness. When you show up late for an appointment, you are saying by your actions that your time is more valuable than the other person's.

Certainly, things may come up that prevent you from meeting your appointment on time. But overall, being prompt in arriving at the time agreed upon is a habit well worth the effort. When you're on time for an appointment, you show your respect for the other person's time.

Being prompt reveals something else about your character. It says, "I'm a person of my word." When you promise to be somewhere at a certain time, your effort to be there is a sign that you keep your promises.

On time, all the time! It'll work for you.

Keep your curfew.

"Always remember the three
B's: be good, be careful,
and be home early."

—Annie Groer

HONOR

Mark thought he had it made. He quietly pushed his car the last few feet into the garage and, ever so gently, eased the garage door down. Tiptoeing into the darkened living room, he went to sit on the couch and take off his shoes. Instead, he sat down on his mother who was asleep on the couch, waiting for him to come home. She screamed! He screamed! And suddenly the whole family was awake. The curfew buster had just been busted!

Why was Mom waiting on the couch? To catch him breaking a curfew? To give him a lecture? No, she was there because she cared about him. Your parents don't set curfew times because they want to spoil your fun. From the moment you were born to the moment you pack and leave for your own home or apartment, they are responsible for your welfare.

Keeping your curfew honors their interest in you. It's a cool way to say "thanks!" for the times they have gone the extra mile for you.

Be a person of integrity.

"When a man makes a promise, he creates an island of certainty in a heaving ocean of uncertainty . . . when you make a promise you have created a small sanctuary of trust within the jungle of unpredictability."

—Lewis Smedes

REPUTATION

You can't buy integrity on the Internet. You get it by being the best possible you. Integrity is having a good reputation—the opinion people have about you based on the personal choices you have made. When those choices are moral, loving, and faith-based, it may be said of you that you are a person of integrity.

You don't gain a good reputation instantly. It's not "microwavable." You get it day by day, month by month, and year by year. You get it decision by decision—individual choices you have made about your attitudes and actions.

If you want to be a person of integrity, start now. Keep your word. Show respect toward others. Live by a high moral standard.

Building a reputation is like building a house. You start with a good design (like the Bible). You gather advice from fellow builders (your family and friends). You set a building schedule (personal goals). You clear the site (put wrongdoing behind you). And then you begin construction.

Say "no" to anything that would harm you or anything that would be harmful to others.

Plan for your future.

"Write it on your heart
that every day is the best
day in the year."

—Ralph Waldo Emerson

PREPARATION

It's not too early to begin thinking about your future. Have you made plans for your continuing education? Do you have a college or vocational school in mind? Are you thinking about military service? You've heard the expression "If you snooze, you lose." That's pretty good advice. Start early. Map out some direction for your post-high school days.

What's your passion? Do you feel like there's a calling on your life? Choose your educational and career goals based on that passion. What are your skills and interests? Choose some life goals that complement that interest—not ones that contradict it.

Thinking about what you'll do after high school will help you to stay focused. For example, if college is in your future, you need to concentrate on your grades. If a sports scholarship is part of that plan, then you need to focus on your sport as well. Make the extra effort. Don't miss practices. Do the extra workouts.

Most of all, seek God's direction. You can trust Him with your future because He's already been there!

Pay attention to the details.

"The ability to listen and follow instructions is a basic life skill with unlimited potential for success."

—David Case

CONCENTRATION

When a popular music group began to plan their world tour, they listed some very specific requirements in their contract—requirements such as how many people the stage could hold, how many technicians they needed to operate the lights, and so forth. To make sure that the contract was read, they added a small but symbolic requirement: The dressing rooms were to be stocked with M & M candy—but no brown ones.

One of the first concert halls looked great. The setup was fantastic, and the show was sold out. But the bowl with the specified candy in the dressing room included brown M & Ms! With great reluctance, the band went on stage. In the middle of the show, the stage collapsed from the weight. Obviously, the concert promoter hadn't read the details. The result was costly repairs to equipment, heavy insurance losses, and the group's refusal to book another concert with the promoter.

Read the fine print. Concentrate on the details. When you pay attention to the small things, the larger ones will fall into place.

Date people you think you could marry.

"Do not be yoked together with unbelievers. For what do righteousness and wickedness have in common? Or what fellowship can light have with darkness?"

—2 Corinthians 6:14

MATURITY

Dating shouldn't be like getting a tooth pulled without an anesthetic. It should be fun—one of the more enjoyable experiences of your life. If you're old enough to date, dating gives you an opportunity to get to know another person on a more personal level.

A lot of people approach dating like someone choosing an item on the Home Shopping Network! They look for something eye-catching. They look at surface stuff: hair color, build, or smile. But what is there about that person that would make you want to spend the rest of your life with him or her?

"Whoa!" you say. "That's not what casual dating is all about." And you're right! Casual dating should be just that: casual. But choosing the qualities in the people we hang out with is the same thing as choosing qualities in our life partners. Do they share your values? What are their life goals? What are their faith commitments?

Being selective about your dating partners is a sign of maturity. Who knows, that first love might be your last one!

Overcome temptation with prayer.

"God does nothing but in answer to prayer."

—John Wesley

RESOURCE

If you were in a battle against someone in a tank and all you had was a pocketknife, would you make an attack? Probably not. You would lack the resources to win such an encounter. But what if you had a friend who flew a fighter jet who made the offer, "Call me if you ever get in a jam"? That's a no-brainer!

There will be times in your life when temptation will come against you like a tank. You will have times when you are tempted to go against your personal values, when you want to give in to your desires no matter what the consequence may be.

At times like that, a pocketknife just won't cut it! You need the power of a jet. God says, "Call me if you get in a jam. I'll help you face the enemy." How do you make the call? Through prayer—talking to God about your concerns.

The next time a "temptation tank" starts toward you, stop! Make the call! Ask God to send some jet fighters from Heaven.

Heaven's resources are better than a Swiss Army knife any day!

Always do the right thing.

"Do right till the stars fall."

—John R. Rice

DECISIVENESS

Placing your order at your favorite sit-down restaurant can be tiring. You are called upon to make a whole bunch of decisions. First, you have to choose a drink order. Next, you choose the main dish. After that, it's the side dish. Then you have to choose the dressing for your salad. If that isn't tiring enough, after you finish the meal, you have to start all over with the dessert tray!

Life is full of decisions. From the moment you wake up to the moment you turn out the light on your nightstand, you are making judgment calls. Making the right calls is important in every area of your life.

Here's a good principle: Always do the right thing. The right thing isn't always the easiest. It's not always the most convenient. And usually the right thing isn't the most popular. But the right thing will always win out over the alternative.

As long as you're forced to make a choice, make the right one.

Learn to be patient.

"With time and patience,
the mulberry leaf becomes
a silk gown."

—Chinese Proverb

PATIENCE

Patience isn't something you inherit like that antique, framed picture of your great-grandmother. Patience is something you earn because of the work you put into it. You learn to be patient, and sometimes the lessons can be pretty painful! That *other* musician gets first chair in the band. Your teacher grades your test on the curve. Your best friend betrays a secret. You come down with the flu on the day of your graduation.

The painful lessons teach you how to "hang in there." They also teach you what to avoid the next time and how to capitalize on your losses.

Learning to be patient means learning how to stand firm. It means facing troubling circumstances with an inner resolve to see them through. It means refusing to be defeated by actions or attitudes that go against you. A patient person has learned how to be agreeable with the people he or she disagrees with. Patience thinks of ways to make the best of the careless and unkind behavior of others and still show a caring concern toward them.

Patience is worth the wait.

Love God with all your heart.

"Jesus replied, 'Love the Lord your God with all your heart and with all your soul and with all your mind. This is the first and greatest commandment.'"

—Matthew 22:37-38

COMMITMENT

Isn't it amazing how animals uncondi-
tionally love their owners? Have you ever
had a dog or a cat that greeted you enthu-
siastically when you walked through the front
door? Your pet seemed to put its whole being
into that welcome. No matter how badly your
day had gone, the welcome was worth it.

God wants us to love Him with that kind of
enthusiasm—nothing-held-back, wholehearted,
and unreserved love. He wants us to love Him
with our total being.

Come to think of it, that's the kind of love He
deserves. The Bible says that God loved us so
much that He gave His only Son. Jesus Christ
was God's total commitment to us when He
gave up His life for us on the cross.

You can't just "sort of" love God and feel any
spiritual vitality. The only relationship with
God that is worth anything is a go-for-the-gold
relationship: all or nothing, 100 percent, a love
with all your heart.

Why not make a total commitment of your
life—everything *you are* to everything *He is*.

About the Author

An international speaker, best-selling author and compassionate teacher, Stan has authored more than 90 books to date. Best sellers include *The Secret Blend; God Has Never Failed Me, but He's Sure Scared Me to Death a Few Times; The Buzzards Are Circling, but God's Not Finished with Me Yet; ReThink Your Life;* his popular Minute Motivators series; and his newest book, *TERRIFIC! Five Star Customer Service.* His books have sold more than three million copies worldwide.

Stan served for 40 years as a pastor, and was named general superintendent emeritus by the Church of the Nazarene denomination. In addition to his writing, he was vice president of John Maxwell's Injoy Ministries, has spoken in 80 countries, and shared the platform with speakers including Zig Ziglar, Jerry Lucas, Rick Warren, Bill Hybels, and Cy Young Award winner R. A. Dickey.

To Contact the Author
Visit www.stantoler.com.